DAYS GONE BY

WAIT UNTIL THE SUN COMES UP

DAYS GONE BY

WAIT UNTIL THE SUN COMES UP

(VOLUME II)

Alexander Obona Hickman

Edited by
Rita 'Caplanis' Howell, MLIS

PAUL SIMPSON HICKMAN

CITI OF
BOOKS

CITIOFBOOKS, INC.
3736 Eubank NE Suite A1
Albuquerque, NM 87111-3579
www.citiofbooks.com
Hotline: 1 (877) 389-2759
Fax: 1 (505) 930-7244

Ordering Information:

Quantity sales. Special discounts are available on quantity purchases by corporations, associations, and others. For details, contact the publisher at the address above.

Printed in the United States of America.

ISBN-13:   Softcover   978-1-962366-41-0
                eBook   978-1-962366-42-7

Library of Congress Control Number: 2023918505

About The Poet

Paul Simpson Hickman

Paul S Hickman was born in Tullahassee, Oklahoma – a small rural African American township. He attended a rural elementary school and graduated from the academic Manual. Training High School in Muskogee, Oklahoma.

During his 26 years of military service, he concurrently completed four college degrees; a post-graduate degree from Vanderbilt University – a graduate degree with Claremont Graduate University-a graduate degree with Golden Gate and a bachelor with LaVerne University in the disciplines of Human Develop and Counseling-Executive Management-Public Administration and Economics. Because of his great skill in job performance, organizational and leadership qualities, he was selected to be the Project Officer for several high-profile military operations in the USA, Greece, and the UK.

In addition- he chaired two Military "Black History Month" Celebrations with University of Oxford academic scholars in attendance in 1981 in the UK, and with US Embassy Staff in attendance in 1986 in Greece. During this period in the UK, he was an adjunct Lecturer of undergraduate courses of Economics, Management, and Business Administration Courses for Embry-Riddle Aeronautical University and the City Colleges of Chicago in the UK.

After his retirement from the military, he returned to Kifisia Greece, and was hired by Southeastern College in Kifisia Greece as an Associate Professor with the duties as the Business Department Coordinator and a lecturer of Management courses at the undergraduate and graduate levels. Further, he was an Adjunct Lecturer as well as the supervisor for three MBA candidates who completed their thesis with the marks of 'Commendable' at the University of Laverne in Greece.

Because of his commitment to bridging cultural gaps, he was inducted into the American-Hellenic Economic Progressive Association [AFIEPA] all in Greece where he was instrumental in arranging a social function for the 1984 American Olympic delegation to Greece with the Honorable Mayor Thomas Bradley-the Mayor of Los Angeles.

After returning to the United States and employed with the State of Maryland as a Disabled Veteran Outplacement Professional for 2 years. While employ there his supervisor made the comment that he did not know what made him tick. With that, he penned and submitted a poem entitled "Spirit Eagle" to the North American Open Poetry contest. His poem was selected for publication by the National Library of Poetry. Then he informed his supervisor that this is who he really was – a poet!

Golden Apple Press published his poem "Simple Things" as the Editor's Choice in their publication entitled "Little Poems-Big Thoughts. He was selected by the National Library of Poetry to submit any one of his poems for their collection of new poems in their "The Best Poets" entitled Best Poems publication. The International Society of Poets rendered him free membership in their society as well as an invitation to become a Distinguished Member of the Society.

Table of Contents

A GLOWING SPARK

Show me thy rituals and
I will show thee thy heart.

If there is a glowing spark, then
there is more to life.

If there is a glowing spark, there
Is a chance to do something good.

So Do It!

FADING AWAY

What was there yesterday
Is no longer.

With time eclipsing
The days, the weeks.

The months, now the years.
All is fading into what?

No longer as exciting
As it was in the yesteryear's.

Now- filled with suspicion
Mistrust, in the halls.

Of the new beginning.
Revealing unfulfilled dreams

Erstwhile needing to be
Remembered for the future.

The dreams were a glowing
Glimpse of what could have
Been – now, they fade.

Melting, slipping into worlds
Of others.

While snow and fires
Cress the day, as noise
Ring into the ears,

We stand waiting....

*GET UP - DO SOMETHING

The way He brings injustice to the surface.
As the viruses swirls into the cores of the

Least of us. We huddle in our homes.
Reviewing the martyring, of some with our

Eyes. Seeing for ourselves the doers. Now, to
Cleanse the disease from the ranks of all

Cultures. While many shudder in fear that
Their ending will be in a place not destined

For them. rushing, out into the streets into
The mist of the viruses of disease and hatred.

Under the protection of Him to move the
Time past 400+ years. Into a clear meadow

Of spirituality and brotherly love.
Get up-Do something! Away! Away...!

SURELY, YOU KNEW - A ROBIN

Ambling, down the street that the Ancient
Greeks trod. Meditating, making the way

to a place of departure. Entering the
Compartment, and oblivious to the world .

A glance, a look into her eyes, without thought,
A soft, curt and glistening voice, "Kalimera"

Pierced the air, interrupting my stoic like
Thoughts. As her face appeared quickly, barely

Visible to the eyes disappearing, perching just
Behind on this journey. The time passes, as

We bade our farewells, departed never to set
Eyes upon the other - my thoughts. The moment

Passes with the winds of the day. Only to appear
At another time and place. Strange, this incident

Reacquainted, in a nanosecond within a sliver of
Time, in a space, an event takes place. There, she's

Walking, passing quickly, a glance, a smiling face
Through the window, rising to greet her. She glides

Through the doors, and the day gives birth to a new
Friend with a purpose.... We, two spirits searching

The cosmos for what! A Robin....

TO, YOU WE GIVE...

To you, we give our life's
long learning. There is no

Place for us, to turn Without
You being there. Reaching

For a way to extinguish this
Picture you have painted

Into our mind's eye. Every turn
Every thought you are always there.

Thinking, at last, being free only
To find that being just

A little deeper than before. To you,
Take our most compassionate feelings and trust....

**PITTER - PATTER

Pitter-patter squirm -roll -squirm.
Small in size as you may be.

Be mindful of your intelligentsia
Capacity. Our foot prints are in

The sands of life for you to step
In, and keep going into the realms
Left for us by our kingdoms.

Kingdoms erased by academicians
Of shallow depths. Unable to fathom

All that was created for us,
and now you. Some think

Too soon -you are Given.
That which is your inheritance.

We are looking out for you.
So you can spread your wings.

And fly to the highest mountain.
Into the forceful winds, and the
Raging seas.

On our backs, you can sit without
Tiring us.

As we cuddle you with our God
Given arms. And you smile- gleefully
Into our eyes.

There we can sense your soul- invisible
To us. But it is there.

Be kind to us as we wither away into
Our eternal resting place.

A DREAM-UNKNOWN

Walking through the narrow street.
Coming upon an old house.
And, going went inside to explain.

Why not to visit an old friend too long.
For having three envelopes to deliver to
A place unknown.

Clutching them tightly. Leaving
In a hurried way.

Exiting the house and turned to
The left, there was an old man.

The women's father! Connected to
An apparatus to his head.

His head with a large piece missing
Had an bald shiny pulsating apparatus.

As she explained this was a new way
To prolong his life. Still leaving hurriedly
Through the street.

Probably, being chased by someone.
Suddenly being lead by a young boy.

Approaching an old building, entering with
The intent to exiting out the back door.

The back door, it was covered with a
Hanging burlap type cloth.

The young boy went through, hesitating
He beckoned me to hurry through.

Near the burlap cloth was a Nun sitting
And weaving, and a priest, and a man,

And a woman taking Holy Communion.
Apologizing for the intrusion and the Nun

Said go ahead and pass. Still clutching the
Three envelopes and exiting the room.

Upon reaching the outside, my tears started
Flowing like water.

Knowing, we had passed through a blessed
Room. And continued the journey to where is

Still unknown. Clutching the three brown old envelopes....

*LOST TALENT

As he sat down with a look of hunger
in his eyes. As I searched, nothing not

Even the lowest. Sensing, a strange and
Different personality from the others.

He glanced up with a gleam in his eyes.
Within minutes, my face was on the white

Paper napkin. Just as quickly as he came
He disappeared for a long, long time.

Thinking, over the months, a talent, this
homeless and hungry person. Drifting, in

A world too busy to care.
As my emotions rose to meet my thoughts.

As quickly as he disappeared, he returned.
Looking deeply hurt in the eyes, My soul

Ripped with sorrow and anger. For I, too,
was with little. As I watched him sipping

Coffee. Knowing the thoughts of his mind
As though they were my own. The world

Would not know his talents. As I gave him
My last. Thinking, his need more important

Than mine. As I walked away. Poured down
The drain, into the sewer, into the sea.

Lost forever! As the tears, began to seep into my
Eyes. I must, I must.

*THESE ARE THE FOUR PAINTINGS PAINTED BY Louis Charles Gaither – 1993 in Prince Charles County, Maryland USA.
The inspiration for the poem in this book entitled – "LOST TALENT".

*Subsequently, I provided the funds for him to purchase art supplies and agreed to purchase all of his paintings. Displayed on the previous page four (4) of them.

**TIS YOU

(Thoughts of The Obamas)

Tis You – who stood like a rock
Of Granite.

Unswayed, by the constant pounding
Of the winds of humanity,

The chilling souls, and the
Fire of dragons.

Now, unweathering streaking into
The Dawn of tomorrow.

As we, the left behind, strive to
Place our footsteps in the soil

Left by you for us to fill in...

STAND TALL

Tried to instill the
Inheritance from the
Ancient Africanoi*.

Powering past the objectives
Of the naysayers.

Tooling the intelligentsia
Handed down into viable

Workmanship of useful growth
Into one of a doer....

A Greek word for the African Female and Male.

THE VIEW OF FIRE*

There the fire starts, raging across
The grassy seas to the worlds of
The lost tribes.

Gathering, them up into a wind swept
Caress and hurls them back to the

Dusty lands-out of deep blue seas.
There they rest until the last days.

None shall be able to touch
Their inner spirit.

From the top of the mountain
Lies a vision as far as the eye
Can see.

No other land will prevail over
This land. As we watch from a distance.

Too far, for many, to short for a few.
As the fires rages on....

*A WALK AWAY

A pleasant day, with the sun glistening
Overhead. Sipping coffee-oblivious
To the worldly things.

Suddenly, a soft voice interrupts
Carried by the gentle winds,

Turning from my book, I looked up
There she stood, radiant, attractive.

Moving closer, a kiss on faces, hello
My good friend from both of us.

Inside, away from the chill of the
Morning. Chatting, the events of
The past days, those of the day.

Sharing our poetic styles, paintings
And poems.

Glancing out the window, she said "that
Scene can be a beautiful painting". To
Which, I agreed.

Being, surrounded by youthful students
Moving noisily about.

Straining to hear each other's voice.
The time passes swiftly with our words
Of events, salient to today's world.

Strolling, down a quiet street, soon
Stopping to say good-by. To part,
Once more....

A kiss on the face, she turns, walking
Briskly away.

Glancing, watching her glide into the
Distant street.

And, she disappears into the world, thinking....

OF THESE AND THOSE DAYS

As we came from, the same mold. Yet some are
Haitians, some Jamaicans, some Dominican

Republic, some Brazilian, some Ethiopian,
some Kenyan, some Ugandan, some Nigerian

Some Sudanese, and yet those of the enslaved
Foregone in America are labeled as "Blacks"!

In these days and those days, but! Are truly
of the Africanoi* cultures.

As we scratch the soils for their bones.

A Greek word for African Female and Male.

**TO STEAL MY LIFE FOR A DAY·2003

Remember, walking down the warehouse aisles
To the abrupt

Stomp of my toe. Thinking that never happened
To me before. As I was a former jogger and ate

The proper foods. Now, my mind seems to not be
Able to solve the simplest logistical issue or

Anticipate probable supply chain delays. What gives?
Traveling, the 9 hours to my new job location on

Weekends a distance far from those dear to my heart.
As her face seemed troubled to me. As wondering why?

The blinking dashboard lights as the journey ends.
And in the early morning to awake with a splitting

Headache. Surmising that this is a serious condition.
Stumbling about to locate the phone, requesting the

Front desk to contact 911. fading in and out and
Decided to take the emergency trip to the nearest

Medical facility via helicopter fading in and out.
Giving the information needed to effect

The surgery and closing my eyes to rest. There comes
A screeching voice cracking through my peaceful

Rest and thoughts [what a peaceful place to be -no noise,
No Challenges, but one regret-never finished my book of

Poetry-as This will be my eternal dream]? Waking up by
My daughter screeching voice " Daddy,! Daddy! Don't leave

Me like this-she was over 900+ miles away. Glancing about,
Realizing the form brick layered walls and lying deep in the

Bottom. The daughter reached to bring me up-to no avail.
Then, the wife-to no avail. Then a strong tanned hand and

Arm covered by a light tan sleeve, reached down and pulled
Me out of my grave. Perplexed, I asked" Why did you do that?

And who are you? "He answered, I am Saint Nicholas-
The New One"! Having been in a coma for 14 days, my

Eyes opened to see my brother and a friend sitting near
My bed. As I expressed to them"Why are you here-there

Was Nothing you could have done"! Then, the days
Afterwards to this day that was almost 20 years ago.

THE AFRICANOI IN RED

-KEVYN

Strolling, to enter the doors to get a beautiful
Greek Orthodox Icon of the Holy Mother framed
As a Valentine Gift.

Strolling, down the aisles, passing rows and rows
Of multicolored flower displays.

Turning, the corner towards the framing table.
There she stood with her back to all of us.

Dressed in an all red outfit with matching red
Shoes. Remembering, the display of red dresses

And accessories in a Greek boutique in Kifisia.
And, within a whisper of the wind, feeling

Compelled to intrude and to greet and
Compliment her on the red outfit and shoes.

As she turned her face with a mask on and
Beyond the mask were the most dazzling brown

Eyes complemented by salt and pepper hair
Gracefully styled.

Giving a courteous, thank you. For the
Compliment. Having never heard the unusual

Name before. She! would never see again?
The day slowly passed,wondering about meeting

This attractive lady on Valentine's Day.
Well! Happy Valentine's Day! Paul! the Africanoi
In Red.

And, there had stood an Africanoi in Red!

POETRY IS FOR DREAMERS

Not a starry night
But a thought of

Why the star?
What is your purpose?

Just sit there shining
And shining. No dancing, no

Movement-really? It is just
A dream of ours. Science has

Told us that stars are moving
At a speed faster than lighting.

Cannot imagine that unless, we
Dream about it.

Poetry is for dreamers.

*A Greek word for African Female and Male

THE MIST IN THE QUIET

There in the land of hero's and beauty
Is a lady. Who moves like a wisp of smoke.

Penetrating all barriers, emerging on the
Side of life that most fail to see.

A forbidden love like a fallen leaf off a tree
Slowly drifting through the gentle breeze.

Bonding with a plethora of others. Moving
over them with differences in hue.

As she glides effortless towards her destiny
In the mist in the quiet of the evening.

There she strolls....

*A COACH AND A PLAYER

To my Lil' Brother-- Coach Taft

The dedication and bonding of both
Permeates the barriers of age and life.

The transplanting of knowledge into the
Player with the grace and skill of an eagle
In a hunt.

The bonding over grows the years current
And past to an unknown level of continuous
Dialogue of both.

Is truth and understanding. As the player goes
Into the Realm of being a "Basketball Jones".

As his coach had been for so many years. His
Coach's love of that 'round pill' supersedes
All other sports on this planet.

As the player watches like a hawk on the prowl
For a victim. Seeing through all of the side noise

And distractions with the focus of a shark. He
Embraces all of the coaches style and techniques

Honing them into a grace likeness of a track star
In a 'Poetry in Motion' likeness with a pure desire
To win and win every time.

As he embraces- his players with a cocoon of love
And respect instilling in them the need to be the

Very best For themselves in each and every challenge.
The days-weeks-months and years pass with grace and

The emerging of a coach- not A player as the cocoon
Dropped away.

All that was ingrained in his soul and heart became as
Granite to be the best and the best is just around the
Corner.

Now! as the epitome of his former coach no longer a
Player- but a coach. As the crowd roars and his players
Push to be as he was with his coach in high school.

Polishing their skills in a diamond like way revealing
The inner beauty of perfection of them as their coach
Not a player for his former coach in high school.

As the years pass, the coach and his coach continue their
Bond as though it is yesterday. As the crowd roars and his
Players .

Smile with love for their coach as he did to his Coach in his
High school days.

With a championship as their target and bound with a steel like
Bond between the players and their coach -they take to the floor.

And the clock starts...

Inspired by the Sun's playing for the NBA championship.

THE ESPRESSO BAR

There it's sitting
Tucked between others

Like it. Strolling
About the colorful decorum

She briskly greets all
With a warming smile

Clothe in simply exotic
Jeans, with leather

Boots the top fringes
Flapping with her every

Step and turn. As modern
Jazz music plays

Softly, in the background.
People walking

Briskly, down the clean
Stone surfaced street.

A fashion show, accentuating
The plethora of

Boutiques encapsulating
The Espresso Bar.

Exotic cars creep along
The narrow street

Exhibiting their unique styles
And models. With

Their little ones riding
Quietly with piercing

Eyes. As a local cat,
Fondly plays with

The small leaf being
gently moved by the

Wind's breath. As
The sun sets quietly

All move to another
Spot to complete

The day at the
Espresso Bar.

Quietly, sitting in the mist
Of the dawn of the eve.

*QUIETLY - WE ROAM AS TIME PASSES

Who knows what lies just over
The horizon. It just keeps moving

Away as we get closer. So we think?
As we have stumbled over sharp rocks

And patches of holes. In our journey to
This day to feel the sweetness in our heart

For the world and those who abhor us.
For as we travel into that distant

Horizon to where....? The pool.
Where the young dash into the
Bubbling and sprinkling waters.

Hopping and skipping around the
Shallow water and playing gleefully

As the tubs of water splashes down
Bring shrieking sounds from their mouths.

As the more advanced ladies thrash
Around in their watery area to the tune

Of music, and in unison with the
Choreographer dancing on the side

Of the pool providing them with
Which direction to take in

Tuning their bodies back into
Good operating form.

Ah ha, if this is roaming as time passes,
Then, it is a very nice and pleasant way to

Roam into the end of the day. As all
Stroll or drive back into the comforts

Of their homes. Gleefully, waiting for
The next day to come and will start all

Over again -roaming as time passes.
As the little ones play gleefully in their

Watery area and the mature ones splash
Around under the guidance of the choreographer.

Day after day as time passes into another epoch.

Inspired by the activity at the local YMCA pool

YOUR AFRICANOI* BLOOD

Your blood flows in our veins. As some
Africanoi are passing through

And some are coming through. After over
400 years "The Post- Africanoi Enslavement

And the Africanoi Diaspora Era in America
And the world. Many cultures reap the creative

Fruits of the Africanoi forefathers and the
Present day Africanoi without one

Scintilla of gratitude. As the inheritors of
The intelligentsia of the Ancient Benin.

Africanoi and all the Ancient Africanoi cultures.
Having, shared these intelligent gifts, With the

World. Their music-science- mathematics-eloquent
Logos-leadership, statesmanship-literature,

Sculptures and sports are a testament of their
Determination to exploit their gifts to their fullest.

No matter the breath or frequency of obstacles
Placed before them. For the Africanoi it is either-
Over-under or through...

Fulfilling the footprint legacies left by the Ancient
Africanoi ancestral cultures. Though, at times

Clouds may cast a shadow on their endeavors.
The Africanoi are still here. Plowing the rows

Towards their destiny to rebuild their humanity and
Share with the world.

Africanoi is a Greek word for Female and Male African.

FOOTPRINTS

Looking back, seeing footprints
In the mud. Things, having been

Done, places gone to and life
Experiences with others.

As the horizon appears ahead of
Our footsteps. Gazing forward

Seeing nothing....But, an empty
Horizon and no footprints

To show us the way to Paradise.
Having missed the essence of the

Moments or being disturbed by the
Impatience of mankind.

Delving, into the traps of wasted time
And into the wasted energy of mankind's

Amusements. While our footprint sinks
Into the mud and life goes on....

REMEMBERING YOU

To My Brother Herbert

Remembering you, when we went
Swimming in dad's pond. I was not

Mud crawling! Remembering you,
When you drove the wagon wheel over

Jo's arm after she fell out of it.
Remembering you, when you threw

My red fire truck out of our burning
House. Remembering you, when someone

Let the 1936 Plymouth roll down, the
Hill into the frozen pond -two mules

Pulled it out. Remembering you and
Rudy playing one on one basketball.

Remembering you always beat him,
And how you two put that small

Tennis ball through the hoop of an empty
Tin can nothing , but net! Remembering

You and the Monarch bicycle you bought
After Rudy had bought a Schwinn bike.

Remembering you calling out got a "carp"
As you came from fishing at the lake crawling

With venomous snakes. Remembering you and
The bricks you threw at the venomous snake

That had climbed up the tree next to the house.
When you got home from school -he almost

Bit me as I was playing self catch in the Yard.
Remembering you and the blue and white 1955

Ford with its broken drive shaft that you repaired.
Remembering you and your beautiful bride named

Sadie who you brought to Muskogee to meet us.
Remembering you and your beautiful daughter

Brenda and you sent us a picture of her at birth.
Remembering you and how proud you were of Tim

JoAnn's husband. And how smart you said he was
Truly he is. But, Joann is smarter and better looking.

Remembering you and your computer that sparked
My children interest in computers -that I have been

Paying for every since. Remembering you
At a health clinic and youg ave me the grand

Tour of the facility in your wheelchair, thinking
Nothing fazes this guy! Remembering you

Remembering you my brother you are my mentor
And hero! You did so much in spite of it all.

Never heard one word of "self-pity"!
Enjoy Heaven! My brother -you have earned it.

EVER SEEN A CATFISH OR A CARP

Ever seen a catfish or a
Carp flopping on the water

Less grass huffing and puffing
For air for the water to be purified

Through their gills into their lungs.
Some men are like the catfish and

The carp. Flopping in earthly zones
Beyond their reach.

Yet trying to lie on a fruitless surface
Made of stone and soil. Constricted by

Their own failure to swim in waters far
From the snares of the fisherman's hook.

As the hook tears into their mouths
And holding on tight with only two

Ways to freedom. One by the
Hand of a gifted man. And the

Other by tearing the flesh and
Breaking free with excruciating pain.

Diving back into the water into
Freedom from the hook of man.

But, so many end up in a place of
Not returning to their former

Life's Trail of their destiny....

*OUR ASIAN SOULMATES

You have been our gracious
Asian neighbors.

Our Vietnam war zone protectors,
Friends And co-workers.

Our Korean IT professional associate.
Our Korean graphic illustrator.

You have been a former interned
Japanese Associate.

And, we have trod with a
Host of acquaintances

From the Asian Nations of
Japan, Korea, Philippines,

Vietnam, China,India, Thailand
Cambodia, Indonesia, Malaysia.

Singapore, and Hong Kong.
All of which have been with

The greatest respect towards
Us and our family and our friends.

To have a vile deed doer martyr
Some of our soulmates is sad and

The work of the evil one.
Who chose a weaker brainwashed
One to do his deed.

May their Memories be Eternal

CLOSER, THAN I KNOW

Softly, the mirror from
Her eyes Gently, slides on

Her face. Like cool drops
Of rain on a early

Quiet spring morning.
As the sun paints, the

Clear blue sky. Silently, her
Tears flow. Cascading on

The slope of her cheeks.
Glistening to kiss and moisten

The day. Piercing her heart,
In search of their essence.

As the sun shine paints,
The clear blue sky,

Her tears flow, silently,
Cascading down the slope

Of her cheeks as the epoch of
The day, slowly close.

She leaves, as the tears....

WHAT CAN WE SAY

To the sauna pals--Corey & Michael

Never thought, to see them as persons to know.
Life moves swiftly, as we grasp to touch a life

Giving candle's flame. Are these times, just a
Reminiscence of the past? The stories from

Yesteryear's?With a slightly different take
But the stories, we have heard before?

Still, making gains on the knowledge of life's
Unfurling demands. As we stumble. Under

The weight of the trials of living coping with
The times, stretching out to capture its essence.

Still growing, demanding self, to stretch further
And further into the realms of the unknown.

Giving praise to God for His Wisdom in Guidance.
Protecting us. Is it really unknown? Or just a fear.

Of the future's demands, It's impact on the world,
As we see it....

DAYS IN AND DAYS OUT

When does it end with our death.
The minutes-hours-days weeks-months-years.

The enslaved toiled without mercy for those who
Controlled our daily movements.

Days In and Days Out

The shear physical and mental pain must be endured
For the Ancestors wrestle with this too. Mental - the
Teachings of the anguish, yet to come - endlessly.

Days In and Days Out

Into the fields, watching over each other with care and love.
Keeping that unseen love intertwined with bitterness

And hatred. Both learned from the ones free to do so
much without regret.

Days In and Days Out

There was no end insight. Some ran away only to
Be returned with bruises and scars. Some whimpered

Like young puppies while other stood tall and erect.
None could wonder without interrogations.

Days In and Days Out

While still chained and living like untamed lions.
Glaring our eyes towards the enslaver who called

Out our action on their parts. The power of the eyes
looking deep into the souls of the enslavers

Raising their fear beyond their belief. As they withheld
The freeing from enslavement when the news passed
Days ago.

Days In and Days Out

The whispers of good news for us. The cuffs and iron around
The neck and ankles were to be taken away.

THE CLOCKS STOPS AFTER 400 YEARS

And the time has come for
The retreat into the caves
From whence we came.

As the Clock Stops.

As the clock stops, and the wind
Blows in from all directions.

As the change is upon us.
With the top down and

Down on top as it has been
Spoken to us.

As The Clock Stops.

As the clock stops, and fear
Grabs the souls of the iniquity

Doer's of deeds. And with the
Vision heard from over the horizon

Whips into our faces
Burning us with the hot wind
Of change.

As the clock stops, then starts
Again with the change done.

And we all stood there in awe...

IT IS ALL ABOUT THE HAIR

Look at this it is. The hair is a protection
For you to duplicate it. I don't think so.

To weave to braid the fluffy. To slick down
To grow like a bush, to shave clear off.

Look at this the hours consumed to
Keep it right. It is all about the hair.

So, remember none others like it.
None near to its texture.

To hate it is to dislike it.
To care for it. It is all about the hair.

To touch, it is not given to others.
The hair is a protection and a

Unifying part of us. Fixing their eyes
Upon it with a scowl on their faces for

That reason ask who? To touch is a
Strong wish by some. To find it spongy

On some, soft and oily or maybe dry and
Brittle on some. It is all about the hair.

As with others, mine is a Gift from God!
It is all about the hair...!

Serenity of These Days

Here among the slightly dense trees.
The voice of a car honking, honking.

As the water fountain gushing noisily.
The chatter of people sitting about

Caressing the mood as the day, peaceful
Noisily quiet.

As the sun blazes above, yet sheltered by
The green vines, and leafy trees.

Tomorrow comes another day filled
With blissfulness and spirited scheming.

Some sitting, sipping frappe, and drinking
Beer, with smokes as the day moves on....

And, we tremble at the outlook of the future
just over the horizon... "Nothing changes

Man still man", and the "Days Gone By"!

PASSING THROUGH, COMING THROUGH

To an Unknown Greek Historian -Leoni

We meet, we talk, we walk,
As time moves on.

Passing through, coming
Through the ages of life.

Searching, for the impossible
dream. As time stops in its place.

Looking to the Sky, as the
Morning speaks, revealing

Passing, coming through life
Knowing, little the future.

Time eclipses all that is a
part of me.

As I pass, you come
Through this time,
This place, this life.

Me, slipping into the wilderness
Of the unknown.

Who know what lies....

YOU GOTTA SEE THIS

You gotta see this.

You gotta live this.

As the generations trod
The streets. As the youth
Trod the streets.

As the cars move through
The streets. With a clear day

No wind the noise of builders
Around the corner.

The gift of the mid-day.

All while we meet for
The clear day.

All while we meet for
The normal day.

All while we wait for
The hug and kisses of
Loved ones.

All while we meet to sit
And sip coffee at the cafe.

All while we wait to feel
The touch of life as it was
In the yesteryear's.

You gotta see this.
You gotta live this

WE STAND AMONG YOU

Being woke. Standing among you. Some must
Feel uncomfortable to grow.

Living in homeostasis is detrimental to the
Common good-for all. Standing among you.

Being woke. Standing among you. Seeing
What you cannot see.

Doing that which you cannot do. Going where
You cannot go. Living as you cannot live.

Who are you? Where did the winds of change
Bring you from?

A mixture of cultures from around the world.
The beauty of the true owners.

How magnificent you appear to us. Having
Waited for a long time. Just to take a seat

Among the living in this hallowed land.
Standing here, seeing you. But, you not

Seeing us. Why? Wondering, why it is so?
Standing here....

A GLIMPSE OF LIFE · FOUR VIEWS

REMEMBERING WHEN

When we were kids and walking down
The street at night in our neighborhoods.

Our biggest fear was the loose dogs.
And today it is the loose humans of all
Cultures.

OUR FATHERS -THE AFRICANOI*

To our fathers as the vain deed doers
Filled with the venom of the evil ones

Touched upon your sacred body and
Trampled it into dust from whence it

Came. As you move to your cross to bear
The sting of barbaric actions.

Your martyrdom will be inherited by your
Seeds planted for the growth of your soul

Into the face of them. Sting their faces and
Rupturing their hearts as their seeds their

Tied to the evil one to reap that which was
Sowed by their fathers.

"Wait Until The Sun Comes Up"!

THE SPIRITS OF THE ANCESTORS LIVES ON

Having heard the stories only little short stories
Of the life under the yoke of other men's will.

Listened to our moms and dads reminiscing
About their youthful days. Days that can only

Go back a few decades then drops off into that
Unknown hollow period of " Lost Ancestors" of

The Africanoi life. Buried beneath the cover revealing
The souls of the Ancient Africanoi carried from the lands.

To a strange place of iniquity. Protect us not as your
Ancestors did for you, but what you must do for us.

For being cheated out of the inheritance, broken like
Wild horses and domesticated into the dreams of others.

WHERE DO WE GO FROM HERE

Over the mountains and across the seas?
To another land to start anew as we bury

The soil of this ravaged one from shore
To shore, from the hills, to the mountains....

AN AFRICAN-AMERICAN LOGO FOR 1981*

Why are you here? What is your
purpose here on earth?

Where are you going? When will
You get there?

Nat Turner, Mary Bethune Cookman,
Carter G. Woodson, Booker T. Washington,

George Washington Carver, Adam Clayton
Powell, Paul Robeson, Jackie, Robinson,

Stokley Carmichael, H "Rap" Brown,
Elijah Muhammad, Muhammad Ali,

James Cleaver, Roy Innis, Shirley Chisholm,

Barbara Jordan and many, many more.
They knew and they were all change agents.

This is not the time to party!
Not the time to joke!

Not the time to feel sorry for ourselves!
Not the time for jealous behavior!
Not the time for gossip!

But the time for reflection!
The time for determination!
The time for learning!

The time for self -renewal of purpose!
That my Africanoi soul mates

Is the primary reason for African-American
History –to remember and get to know
Those who came before us.

Today, We ask you to look deeply
Into your spirit, beyond the material

Aspects of the young people who will
Come before you.

You are and they are the products
Of our ancestors.

You have a hard long challenging
Journey ahead of you with many
Obstacles before you.

But! the hard roads will not go away
You must conquer them.

As a guide, leaving with you the map
From the youth of our home towns.

Of the 1960's protest and Civil Rights
Movement. SESEP- Spiritual, Emotional,

Social, Educational and Physical endeavors
To accomplish.

Keep these balanced, and you will find
your purpose in life.

And for courage, we give you this prayer
"Oh God grant me the Serenity

To accept the things that I cannot change...
The Courage to change the things I can

And the wisdom to know the difference".
-Saint Francis of Assisi [Until we come to know the philosophy of our Africanoi Ancestors]

* As I took the reins as the Chairperson for the African-American History Month [in this meeting only
one came-myself].

INTO THE REALM OF DISCOURSE

To Irene, My Daughter

Finally, off on the long journey
To a familiar land. Fearful, yet

Unafraid of the long wait to see her.
As remembered, surely not the same

As it was you left. But will still caress
The spirit with renewed freshness.

To see souls wondering, lost in a morass
Of ideas seeking, a solution for the pain,

That follows. The poor judgments, grasping
For answers from other

Lands. While looking far way, will not provide
Them. The answer, nor the good life again.

Life passes, without clear thoughts or dreams.
To shed light for ideas, trod into a

New epoch. As the cosmos rushes....
To escape that which is not to be escaped

And the windows slowly close....

DANCING TOWARDS THE ANGELS

And having loved so many
Of you. Some more than others.

But loved just the same.
Some went too soon as they

Were Dancing Towards the
Angels. Whirling around us,

The left behind to live without
Them to touch and hold.

As they were Dancing towards
The Angels. Some waiting, their

Turn to Dance Towards The Angels,
And yet some will not get the thrill

Of whirling through the Heavenly
Skies. Wondering, when the day comes

For their arrival to take them to the
Dance Towards The Angels.

With so many thunderous interruptions
All around making the "Dance" so strenuous

For the spirit. Encountering, obstacles to
Battle thrown from so many sources,

Catching many off guard. With God's
Desire for Patient, Wisdom and Obedience,

As this will be the last of the dancing.
Being summoned, to the furthermost point

In the Holy House in the mist of the
Glorifying the Water.

Hearing the young lady's chanting voice
That has grown far from a child's voice into

A solid strong spirited, gifted one.
Her chanting tones are as pure and

Clear as a canary's songs. Trekking!
On the paths laid out before them a

Journey towards the Dancing...
Arriving! at the next epoch for

"Dancing Towards The Angels".

WITHIN ME LIES A DREAM STORY*

Do you want me to tell it to you?
Will you listen? Probably not?

Well, let me say this. Once upon
A time...Ham or Cush.

While in the que to take Holy
Communion having a choice to

Go the Priest on the left
Or the right. but, there

Stood an unknown Monk [to me]
In the center. So deciding to

Go to him. Approaching to
Utter my name.

He asked of me-first! "Paul!
Which one convinced you to

Become an Orthodox to marry
Maria-Anna? Ham or Cush"?

I said Cush- reluctantly.
AS THE DREAM ENDED HERE

In researching the names
Of Ham and Cush learning

That Ham was the son of Noah and
Cush was the son of Ham.

In the Old Testament there
In the information.

Reading that the Cushites were
A dark skinned people.

Whose King possessed thousands
And thousands

Of men with 300 chariots...
Asa asked God to help him

Fight against the Cushites.
The Cushites were defeated

And their Kingdom destroyed.
The Cushites/Ethiopians lived

South of Egypt. And moved around
Many areas....

*As this a dream in answering my concern about the validity of the documentary of Cleopatra III.
Then I researched*

THE DAWN SETS A NEW HORIZON - TOMORROW

Now, Where for the - Obama's

Breaking, through the darkness stretching
Across the sky.

Sailing, over the grass, the ground, the
Trees, the mountains, then the ocean.

As, some awake to see the bright light of
The sun. But, many have slept through

The thunderous silent roar of the Dawn.
As Dawn sets a new horizon far away - Today.

And, it moves swiftly before our very eyes.
While many sleep, missing this majestic wonder.

Now What....?

THE DAYS TO COME

As we stand here in the dawn
Of the iniquity of man.

Solemn towards the passing
Of the glow of the sun light.

Kissing the waves of the seas
And garnering substance

From the mountains, As we
stand here.

As the trees bend and sway
With the winds of change.

As the thunder roars, and the
Lightning cracks noisily in

The cloudy sky. The Days To
Come. As we stand here.

Immersed in the ways of man
That leads to nowhere for so

Many. As we wait for others
to lead us to where?

Grand parents are gone. Parents
Are gone.

As we stand here waiting for
The Days to Come....